Study Guide for Abduction: How Liberalism Steals Our Children's Hearts And Minds

Steve Feazel & Dr. Carol M. Swain

ISBN 9781522055273

Contact Information:

Carol Swain Enterprises, LLC
P.O. Box 1385
Brentwood, TN 37024
E-mail: carolswainenterprises@gmail.com

Scripture quotations are taken from the English Standard Version. © 2001 by Crossway Bibles, a division of Good News Publishers.

Table of Contents

Preface

After listening to your feedback, Steve and I
decided to create a resource guide for individuals
and organizations who would like to use *Abduction*
to alert a larger audience about the dangerous
choices confronting America's children. We
provide chapter-by-chapter questions suitable for
classroom use, book clubs, and other discussion
forums. Group leaders can select one or more
questions or exercises from each chapter for weekly
discussion or they can modify the questions to make
them more suitable for your particular group's age
and educational level.

Acknowledgments

We owe a great debt to Dr. Jeanie Roberson who worked diligently on this study guide and offered her insights and wisdom at every stage of development. In addition, I owe a debt to the Brentwood Garden Club for selecting and organizing one of the first group studies of *Abduction*. Diane Birnbaum, Debbie Deaver and Debbie Goodloe are owed special thanks. I am also indebted Kimberly MacNeill, to Women, at Forest Hills Baptist Church and Faith Murphy who selected *Abduction* for a study group.

Chapter 1:
The Enemy Revealed

Ephesians 6:10-13 Finally, be strong in the Lord and in the strength of his might. Put on the whole armor of God, that you may be able to stand against the schemes of the devil. For we do not wrestle against flesh and blood, but against the rulers, against the authorities, against the cosmic powers over this present darkness, against the spiritual forces of evil in the heavenly places. Therefore, take up the whole armor of God, that you may be able to withstand in the evil day, and having done all, to stand firm.

Revelation 12:12 Therefore, rejoice, O heavens and you who dwell in them! But woe to you, O earth and sea, for the devil has come down to you in great wrath, because he knows that his time is short!"

1. A quote by John F. Kennedy, stated at the beginning of chapter one, says that "the great enemy of the truth is very often not the lie… but the myth." What does this statement mean? Give an example from current events that proves this to be true.

2. According to Feazel and Swain, the first step in winning the war is to "know your enemy." Compare and contrast traditional morality with the new morality. Describe

four distinct differences between the two ideologies.

3. Contrary to the accounts of biased historical revisionists, Feazel and Swain provide multiple excerpts from historical documents, written by people instrumental in the founding of America, that show they believed that traditional morals were foundational for the republic they would create. Choose several of the excerpts and describe how they provide insight into how these people conceived of government and the guidelines upon which it should be founded. What consistently stands out as being essential to liberty and happiness? Examine other early American documents and share examples that support or oppose this view.

4. As the New Morality grows in influence, changes in our society are clearly evident. Allow your mind to fast forward to a time where every evidence of traditional morality has disappeared, what would a society based completely on the New Morality and its championing forces of humanism and material naturalism look like?

5. What is the danger of basing our legal system on sociological law? How does the

belief that law descends from God serve as protection for mankind? Describe specific examples that prove that logical constraints prevent societal chaos.

6. The basic principle of Joseph Fletcher's book, *Situation Ethics* (1966), is that "there is nothing which is universally right or universally wrong; there is nothing which is intrinsically good or intrinsically bad." What is the danger of this belief?

7. The Constitution prohibits the establishment of a national church, but it never intended to separate religious faith from political life. The Founding Fathers believed that religious faith not only forms the basis of our Constitution, but also is critical to our ability to endure as a free society. How does the demand of the liberal Left for a purely secular government oppose the original intent of our Founding Fathers? What are the consequences of their demand?

Chapter 2:
Exposing the Myth

Psalm 10:2-12 In arrogance the wicked hotly pursue the poor; let them be caught in the schemes that they have devised. For the wicked boasts of the desires of his soul, and the one greedy for gain curses and renounces the LORD. In the pride of his face the wicked does not seek him; all his thoughts are, "There is no God." His ways prosper at all times; your judgments are on high, out of his sight; as for all his foes, he puffs at them. He says in his heart, "I shall not be moved; throughout all generations I shall not meet adversity." His mouth is filled with cursing and deceit and oppression; under his tongue are mischief and iniquity. He sits in ambush in the villages; in hiding places he murders the innocent. His eyes stealthily watch for the helpless; he lurks in ambush like a lion in his thicket; he lurks that he may seize the poor; he seizes the poor when he draws him into his net. The helpless are crushed, sink down, and fall by his might. He says in his heart, "God has forgotten, he has hidden his face, he will never see it." Arise, O LORD; O God, lift up your hand; forget not the afflicted.

1. Explain the difference between the interpretations of the Establishment Clause of the First Amendment by the New Morality versus the Traditional Morality.

Which do you think is the correct
interpretation and why?

2. How does Alexis de Tocqueville's quote on
page 59 substantiate the argument that our
Christian heritage was key to America's
success?

3. Describe how the New Morality has
distorted the original meaning of Thomas
Jefferson's phrase "thus building a wall of
separation between Church and State."
When placed in context, what was his
original intent? Are the words "separation of
church and state" in the Constitution or in
any official documents related to the
establishment of the United States of
America? What other actions by Jefferson,
when he was President of the United States,
contradict the claim that he believed in a
wall of separation that prevented any
interference from religion?

4. Page 70 and 71 list judgments handed down
by the courts based on a misinterpretation of
the separation of church and state. These
court decisions are evidence that the New
Morality has gained much ground in the
culture war. How are supporters of
traditional morality fighting back? Visit
https://aclj.org (American Center for Law

and Justice) and http://www.frc.org (Family Research Council). What are these organizations doing to reverse the damage caused by the New Morality? What other organizations are leading the battle against the New Morality?

5. Construct a defense for the belief that our Founding Fathers included the "establishment clause" in the First Amendment for the sole purpose of preventing Congress from making a law to declare a particular sect or denomination as the official national church. Provide additional evidence that the phrase "or prohibiting the free exercise thereof" restricted Congress from being intrusive on the practices of religion, while still allowing religion to influence the government.

6. Consider Jefferson's concerns regarding the danger that the judiciary branch was not held accountable to an electorate. How have these concerns come to fruition in the influence of the New Morality on our present judicial system?

7. Research and investigate the Vacation Liberty School. What is their mission? What is included in the curriculum? Do you know of any churches or organizations that have

utilized this curriculum in your area? What steps would be required to offer this curriculum through your church or organization?

Chapter 3:
Public Schools: Ground Zero

Luke 17:1-2 And he said to his disciples, "Temptations to sin are sure to come, but woe to the one through whom they come! It would be better for him if a millstone were hung around his neck and he were cast into the sea than that he should cause one of these little ones to sin.

Proverbs 22:6 Train up a child in the way he should go; even when he is old he will not depart from it.

1. Christianity is not welcome in public schools, even in places where other religions are accommodated. Is this true in your area of the country? Share examples of this from personal experience and/or local news outlets. If the point is to ban all religions from the public scene where tax dollars are at work, why is there increased inclusion of Islamic studies in public schools? Is this a double standard?

2. What is one of the main issues with using the First Amendment to intervene in state law? Should the Supreme Court have power over religious activities in individual states? Is there a way for the legislative or executive branches of government to limit the reach of

Supreme Court decisions?

3. What was problematic about the court decision in the 1962 case of *Engel v. Vitale*, regarding the "constitutionality" of prayer in public schools? Why from 1789 until 1962 was prayer acceptable in public schools? How can concerned citizens use the "free exercise" clause to argue for an individual child's rights to pray out loud in a school cafeteria, or before an athletic event, or in a student-led after school Bible study?

4. Examine some of the textbooks used in your local public schools. (Public libraries usually have copies of the textbooks adopted by the public schools in their area). Is there evidence of bias and censorship? Is the Christian influence on our nation's history mentioned? What novels and stories are included as representative of American literature? Is there a rationale provided for what is included?

5. Is "death education" being offered in your local school district? Speak to local school officials and ask for their opinions on the subject. According to the American Academy of Child & Adolescent Psychiatry (October, 2013) suicide is the third leading cause of death for 15-to-24-year-olds, and

the sixth leading cause of death for 5-to-14-year-olds. Considering this fact alone, do adolescents have the intellectual and emotional ability to use their own judgment in deciding whether to live or die?

6. The student population of the United States for the fall of 2016 was composed of 50.4 million students in public elementary and secondary schools, 5.2 million students in private elementary and secondary schools, and 1.5 million students under homeschool umbrella organizations. From these statistics, it is obvious that public schools are the principal method that our nation has chosen to educate our children. Giving up on public schools is not an option. How can we address the issues that have been raised in this chapter and ensure that public schools are designed to help students obtain the skills and knowledge needed to make a living and function as productive citizens?

Chapter 4:
Sexy Kids

1 Timothy 4:12 Let no one despise you for your youth, but set the believers an example in speech, in conduct, in love, in faith, in purity.

Hebrews 13:4 Let marriage be held in honor among all, and let the marriage bed be undefiled, for God will judge the sexually immoral and adulterous.

1. At what age is sex-education introduced in your school district? Review the books and curriculum used at each grade. Are the materials appropriate for the intellectual and emotional development of the children at each grade level? Is abstinence the main emphasis? What input and amount of control do parents have regarding what their children are exposed to?

2. Talk to your children, grandchildren, or other adults with children to discover what is taking place in local schools regarding desensitization to the LGBT lifestyle. What actions can you take to reverse and neutralize the militant agenda of the LGBT community in public schools?

3. Is the curriculum designed by the Sexuality Information and Education Council of the United States (SIECUS) being used in your

local schools? Look at the examples, on pages 102-104, of what they teach at each age level. Many religions, in addition to Christianity, would be opposed to this content. Religious beliefs aside, do you believe that these topics are developmentally appropriate for children at each of these age levels? Why or why not? Speak with Christian counselors for advice about getting age-appropriate sex-education materials. Contact Focus on The Family or other Christian organizations to find more information regarding materials to equip parents for educating their children about sex.

4. What does the Bible say about homosexuality and sex outside of marriage? Study the context and original language of the verses pertaining to these topics. How would you discuss this with someone that has been told that the Bible does not condemn homosexuality or sex outside of marriage?

5. How should Christians respond to people that are struggling with homosexuality, transgender dysphoria, or same-sex attraction? Use resources such as Exodus Global Alliance (www.exodusglobalalliance.org) and Parents

and Friends of Ex-Gays (www.pfox.org) for information on how to support children and adults struggling with these issues. Share your findings with your group and brainstorm ways to provide information to other churches and people that support traditional morals. Should this information be presented in public schools? What can be done to convince school boards and administrators, that if students are presented with the pro-LGBT agenda, they should also be given the opposite view?

Chapter 5:
Music Hits a Sour Note

Psalm 146:1-2 Praise the LORD! Praise the LORD, O my soul! I will praise the LORD as long as I live; I will sing praises to my God while I have my being.

Ephesians 5:17-19 Therefore do not be foolish, but understand what the will of the Lord is. And do not get drunk with wine, for that is debauchery, but be filled with the Spirit, addressing one another in psalms and hymns and spiritual songs, singing and making melody to the Lord with your heart.

1. Aristotle stated that "Music has a power of forming the character." Much of music aimed at teenagers today glamorizes promiscuous sex, drug and alcohol use, rape and even murder. Do you agree with Aristotle and if so, how do you think popular music is affecting our teenagers?

2. The late federal judge Robert Bork argued that interpretation of the First Amendment has morphed from the protection of the expression of ideas to the protection of self-expression regardless of how vulgar and profane the self-expression is. Have we allowed freedom of expression to go too far? Do an internet search on the psychological effect of violent and vulgar lyrics. Share

what you find with others in your group. Do you agree that society has a right to constrain activity that puts itself at risk? Could we apply the same logic behind our drug laws to create laws that restrict music that results in high-risk behavior by those who listen to it?

3. Music-industry executive, Danny Goldberg, defended gangsta rap (known for its violence, vulgarity, and degradation of women) by saying that "it is a direct descendant of the gangster movies of the 1930s and 1940s, the TV Westerns of the 1950s, and critically acclaimed films like *The Godfather*." Do you agree with Goldberg? Why or why not?

4. The music industry, along with the film industry, believe that censorship should not apply to them and that they are protected by the First Amendment. How are they hypocritical in this belief?

5. Chapter five ends with an example of a group of college women that took action against the rap music genre. What other things can be done to make the music industry more accountable for the music they are producing? How can we encourage writers and musicians to produce positive

and inspiring music with a wholesome message?

Chapter 6:
Big Screen, Little Value

Philippians 4:8 Finally, brothers, whatever is true, whatever is honorable, whatever is just, whatever is pure, whatever is lovely, whatever is commendable, if there is any excellence, if there is anything worthy of praise, think about these things.

1. Does violence in movies motivate children to commit acts of violence? Provide examples to support your answer.

2. To what degree do you think Hollywood affects our culture? Does it have any positive effects? What are some of its negative effects? What is the best way to put pressure on Hollywood to create more family-friendly movies?

3. What steps can we take to help our children become discerning media consumers?

4. Brainstorm what can be done to encourage and support filmmakers, such as the Kendrick brothers and Dinesh D'Souza.

5. Become familiar with Mr. Baehr's *Movieguide* (www.movieguide.org) and Focus on the Family's *Plugged In*

(www.pluggedin.com). The *Movieguide* is the family guide to movies and entertainment. Their mission is to "redeem the values of the entertainment industry, according to biblical principles, by influencing industry executives and artists." *Plugged In* reviews movies, TV, music, games and books. Their mission is "to shine a light on the world of popular entertainment while giving families the essential tools they need to understand, navigate, and impact the culture in which they live." What can you do to make more people aware of these resources and encourage their use?

6. Read the Summit Medical Group's finding on the harmful impact of R-rated movies on children, located at http://www.summitmedicalgroup.com/library/pediatric_health/hhg_r-rated_movies/ Share other books and articles about methods of protecting our children from harmful media with your group.

Chapter 7:
Invader in a Box

Romans 6:1-14 What shall we say then? Are we to continue in sin that grace may abound? By no means! How can we who died to sin still live in it? Do you not know that all of us who have been baptized into Christ Jesus were baptized into his death? We were buried therefore with him by baptism into death, in order that, just as Christ was raised from the dead by the glory of the Father, we too might walk in newness of life. For if we have been united with him in a death like his, we shall certainly be united with him in a resurrection like his. We know that our old self was crucified with him in order that the body of sin might be brought to nothing, so that we would no longer be enslaved to sin. For one who has died has been set free from sin. Now if we have died with Christ, we believe that we will also live with him. We know that Christ, being raised from the dead, will never die again; death no longer has dominion over him. For the death he died he died to sin, once for all, but the life he lives he lives to God. So you also must consider yourselves dead to sin and alive to God in Christ Jesus. Let not sin therefore reign in your mortal body, to make you obey its passions. Do not present your members to sin as instruments for unrighteousness, but present yourselves to God as those who have been brought from death to life, and your members to God as instruments for righteousness. For sin will have no dominion over you, since you are not under law but under grace.

1. Chapter seven begins with a quote by Ravi Zacharias: "Television has been the single greatest shaper of emptiness." Do you agree or disagree with the quote? Support your answer.

2. Feazel and Swain state that "We might regard our TV sets as electronic windows to the world, but the New Morality sees it as an avenue of opportunity by which to invade our homes." What makes television unique and more dangerous than movies?

3. Do violence and sexual content in TV programs lead to more violence and sexual promiscuity in real life? What are some of the cumulative effects of repeated exposure to TV violence? Conduct an internet search for research studies that answer these questions. Share your findings with the group.

4. One of the common responses to complaints about the content of TV programs is, "If you don't like it, turn it off." Why is this answer not as simple as it appears? Why does making your own choice to "turn it off" not

stop the influence of TV violence, sexual perversion, and vulgarity on you and your family?

5. TV shows originally were relatively apolitical, pro-American, and reflected a traditional view of social norms. Television today follows the politics of the left and the New Morality affecting the way sex, authority, and even good and evil are seen. Think about television programs you watch regularly. Share examples of how the New Morality is reflected in these shows. How do you address this with your children? How do you counteract and reverse the influence this constant barrage has on your mind?

6. Visit the website of The Parents Television Council (http://w2.parentstv.org). The mission of the PTC is "to protect children and families from graphic sex, violence and profanity in the media, because of their proven long-term harmful effects...to provide a safe and sound entertainment media environment for children and families across America." Read about their current campaigns and consider ways you and your group can get involved.

Chapter 8:
Children, Stolen and Gone

1 Thessalonians 4:3-8 For this is the will of God, your sanctification: that you abstain from sexual immorality; that each one of you know how to control his own body in holiness and honor, not in the passion of lust like the Gentiles who do not know God; that no one transgress and wrong his brother in this matter, because the Lord is an avenger in all these things, as we told you beforehand and solemnly warned you. For God has not called us for impurity, but in holiness. Therefore, whoever disregards this, disregards not man but God, who gives his Holy Spirit to you.

Psalm 51:10 Create in me a clean heart, O God, and renew a right spirit within me.

1. Lieutenant Colonel Dave Grossman contends that violent video games are having the same effect on kids as the military's training-to-kill programs have on new recruits. He points out that "the data linking violence in the media to violence in society is superior to that linking cancer and tobacco." The Mothers Against Videogame Addiction and Violence organization is dedicated to "educating parents about video game addiction and violence in underground

video game cultures." Visit their website (http://www.mavav.org) to become more aware of what research says about the detrimental effects of violent and sexually explicit video games on children. Share your findings with the group. If you have children or grandchildren, what methods have you used to put parameters on their use of video games and other electronic devices? What challenges have you faced in implementing and enforcing these controls?

2. Read *The Impact of Pornography on Children* by the American College of Pediatricians, https://www.acpeds.org/the-college-speaks/position-statements/the-impact-of-pornography-on-children. Discuss the negative effects of pornography on children and people in general. What actions are recommended to help protect your children from exposure to pornography?

3. Organizations, such as the North America Man/Boy Love Association, are attempting to end restrictions placed on sex, as long as both parties are consenting. This is the next step in the progression of our society's path to destruction. We have moved from being forced to accept the normality of sex before marriage to sex between people of the same gender and now to sex between adults and

children. What is the legal definition for age of consent? Do children and teenagers have the intellectual and emotional ability needed to weigh the consequences of participating in sexual intimacy? Research has thoroughly documented the effects of childhood sexual abuse. Where is the line between abuse and consenting sex when children can be easily bribed, manipulated or intimidated? There are many articles on protecting children from sexual predators. Do an internet search and research this topic. Share your findings with your group.

4. Discuss the changes in our society, in the last fifty years, brought on by the sexual revolution. Is our society better because of it? Support your answer with examples.

5. Read and study the forty-two Bible verses that apply specifically to raising godly children, available at www.open-bible.info/topics/raising_children. Analyze and synthesize these verses into major principles and discuss how to implement these with your children or grandchildren. Find ways to share this information on Facebook and other social media outlets.

6. Have you considered homeschooling your children? Find out what homeschool

umbrella groups operate in your area. Speak to parents that homeschool. Ask them to discuss the pros and cons of homeschooling with your group.

Chapter 9:
Higher Learning and Lower Values

Romans 1:18-32 For the wrath of God is revealed from heaven against all ungodliness and unrighteousness of men, who by their unrighteousness suppress the truth. For what can be known about God is plain to them, because God has shown it to them. For his invisible attributes, namely, his eternal power and divine nature, have been clearly perceived, ever since the creation of the world, in the things that have been made. So they are without excuse. For although they knew God, they did not honor him as God or give thanks to him, but they became futile in their thinking, and their foolish hearts were darkened. Claiming to be wise, they became fools, and exchanged the glory of the immortal God for images resembling mortal man and birds and animals and creeping things. Therefore, God gave them up in the lusts of their hearts to impurity, to the dishonoring of their bodies among themselves, because they exchanged the truth about God for a lie and worshiped and served the creature rather than the Creator, who is blessed forever! Amen. For this reason, God gave them up to dishonorable passions. For their women exchanged natural relations for those that are contrary to nature; and the men likewise gave up natural relations with women and were consumed with passion for one another, men committing shameless acts with men and receiving in themselves the due penalty for their error. And since they did not see fit to acknowledge God, God gave them up to a debased mind to do what ought not to be done. They were filled with all manner of unrighteousness, evil, covetousness, malice. They are full of envy, murder, strife, deceit, maliciousness. They are gossips, slanderers, haters of God, insolent, haughty, boastful, inventors of evil, disobedient to parents, foolish, faithless, heartless, ruthless. Though they know God's decree that those who practice such things deserve to die, they not only do them but give approval to those who practice them.

1. Feazel and Swain state that "changes have come to colleges and universities across the nation in the last forty years that have not been good for the country or the future of the children we send to them…When you send a kid to a state university or private college today, they become direct targets of the New Morality." Share examples of the changes that you have seen take place in colleges and universities through your own experience and stories that have been shared with you.

2. Read the article *The Coddling of the American Mind* by Greg Lukianoff and Jonathan Haidt (https://www.theatlantic.com/magazine/arch

ive/2015/09/the-coddling-of-the-american-mind/399356/). What do the authors say are the effects of this protectiveness on the students? What do they suggest is the cure?

3. Visit the website of The Young America's Foundation (http://www.yaf.org). How is this organization trying to equip conservative students to win back their college campuses? What are some of their current projects? How can you encourage the college group at your church to become involved in this organization? How can you become involved and support this organization?

4. What are some of the short and long-term consequences both male and female students are experiencing because of the casual sex environment of colleges and universities? Instead of providing guidelines and parameters to help students make wise decisions regarding dating and sex, how are colleges and universities aiding and abetting sexual activity?

5. Conservative faculty and students, who find themselves discriminated against and attacked, can reach out to the Foundation for Individual Rights in Education (FIRE). Visit their website (https://www.thefire.org) and

familiarize yourself with their mission and what they do to carry out their mission. What ways can you support this organization and others like it?

6. What can parents do to help their children make the best choice when deciding which college or university to attend? Once they have made the choice, what other things can parents do to help prepare their children for what they will experience in college? What can parents do to help their children once they are attending college?

Chapter 10:
Black Robes Bring Dark Days

Isaiah 47:10-11 You felt secure in your wickedness, you said, "No one sees me"; your wisdom and your knowledge led you astray, and you said in your heart, "I am, and there is no one besides me." But evil shall come upon you, which you will not know how to charm away; disaster shall fall upon you, for which you will not be able to atone; and ruin shall come upon you suddenly, of which you know nothing.

Deuteronomy 16:18 "You shall appoint judges and officers in all your towns that the LORD your God is giving you, according to your tribes, and they shall judge the people with righteous judgment."

1. The role of the judicial branch as dictated by the Constitution, is to interpret the law, settle disputes, and serve as a watchdog for balancing the separate branches of government. Further, the judiciary was to ensure that the national government respected the autonomy granted state governments under the Tenth Amendment. Is the judicial branch fulfilling their role? Give examples to support your answer.

2. Supreme Court justices are directed to base their decisions on the Constitution and precedence set by decisions in similar court

cases. Why have our Supreme Court justices sought guidance from the courts of other countries? How can a justice assume that the cultures and values of another country automatically fit our country and then dare to copy their decision? What is the motivation of the justices that choose to do this?

3. Where can you find out about qualifications and previous decisions of potential nominees to the federal bench? Pray for wisdom and guidance for our President as he nominates people to fill these positions and for the Senate as they vote for them. What else can you do to encourage the President and Senators to nominate and vote for people that are pro-America, pro-traditional values, and pro-Constitution?

4. Visit the websites of some or all of the following organizations: Eagle Forum (eagleforum.org), the Family Research Council (https://www.frc.org), the Heritage Foundation (www.heritage.org), American Center for Law and Justice (https://aclj.org), and American Values (https://www.ouramericanvalues.org). Sign up for newsletters from these organizations that will keep you informed about what is happening in Congress and in other relevant

areas of American life that pertain to traditional values and individual liberty. Organize and sponsor events that bring representatives from these organizations to come and speak in your area.

5. Get involved by writing letters, making phone calls, writing op-eds, and organizing protests against candidates and nominees who stand for principles that run contrary to traditional values and principles.

Chapter 11:
Fighting Back

2 Chronicles 7:14 If my people who are called by my name humble themselves, and pray and seek my face and turn from their wicked ways, then I will hear from heaven and will forgive their sin and heal their land.

1 Corinthians 9:24 Do you not know that in a race all the runners run, but only one receives the prize? So run that you may obtain it.

Hebrews 12:1-2 Therefore, since we are surrounded by so great a cloud of witnesses, let us also lay aside every weight, and sin which clings so closely, and let us run with endurance the race that is set before us, looking to Jesus, the founder and perfecter of our faith, who for the joy that was set before him endured the cross, despising the shame, and is seated at the right hand of the throne of God.

1. Since the 1960s, the New Morality and the liberal Left have made great advances. The New Morality affects every sphere of our lives. What are some reasons behind the successes of the New Morality?

2. The cultural war that is raging between Traditional Morality and the New Morality has been clearly defined throughout this book. We can no longer stand on the

sidelines and hope for the best. Our children and our nation are at stake. What are some of the specific ways that we can join in the fight?

3. The cultural war is a battle for the soul of the nation. The Liberal Left claims that you cannot legislate morality. Why is this nonsense? What is the real issue? Why does it make a difference what morality is based on?

4. Why is the term progressive an oxymoron when used in reference to the Liberal Left?

5. Although voting in elections is a crucial part of winning the war against the New Morality, another essential piece is recapturing the culture. Feazel and Swain explain, "Wherever the culture war is being waged, we need to be in that area making a difference. We need to discard the bunker mentality that has encompassed many traditional moralists and evangelicals." What are some specific strategies we can implement to recapture our culture? What actions will you take to help protect our nation's most valuable resource, its children?

6. Encourage your church and Sunday school superintendent to offer classes in apologetics for teens and middle-school children so they will be equipped to respond to the secularists who would mock their faith and corrupt their values. Follow this link to Sean McDowell's website for a list of apologetics resources for teens (http://seanmcdowell.org/blog/what-are-the-best-apologetics-resources-for-students).

Made in the USA
Monee, IL
28 October 2020